10-MINUTE
BRAIN
WORKOUT

Brain-Training Tricks, Riddles and Puzzles
to Exercise Your Mind

GARETH
MOORE

Introduction, puzzles and
solutions by Gareth Moore

Illustrations by Nikalas Catlow

Dr Gareth Moore is the author of a wide range
of puzzle books for both children and adults.
He gained his PhD at Cambridge University in
the field of machine intelligence, later using his
experience in computer-software research and
development to produce the first book
of kakuro puzzles published in the UK.
He has a wide range of media interests and
also runs several websites, including the
online sudoku site **www.dosudoku.com**.

Other titles by the author:
The Kids' Book of Kakuro
The Kids' Book of Hanjie
The Kids' Book of Number Puzzles
The Kids' Book of Sudoku: Challenge Edition
The Book of Kakuro
The Book of Japanese Puzzles
The Book of Hanjie
Quick Kakuro
The Book of Hitori
The 10-minute Brain Workout

KIDS'
10-MINUTE
BRAIN
WORKOUT

Brain-Training Tricks, Riddles and Puzzles
to Exercise Your Mind

GARETH MOORE

Buster
Books

First published in Great Britain in 2006 by Buster Books,
an imprint of Michael O'Mara Books Limited,
9 Lion Yard, Tremadoc Road,
London SW4 7NQ

ISBN 978-1-905158-53-9

INTRODUCTION

Kids' 10-Minute Brain Workout contains ninety ten-minute brain workouts that will maximize your mental powers!

Did you know that your brain has up to double the learning power of an adult's brain? As you get older, parts of your brain that you don't use regularly begin to fade away – just the same as the muscles in your body become weaker if you don't exercise.

Kids' 10-Minute Brain Workout is packed full of short puzzles that will help you train your brain. There is one complete brain workout on every page, and there are many different types of workout too. By doing a wide range of mental activities you'll get to exercise different areas of your brain and keep your mental powers in tip-top condition. Try to do one or two pages a day and to finish each page in under ten minutes.

Kids' 10-Minute Brain Workout will help improve your memory, language skills, numeracy, concentration, and visual and spatial awareness. Upgrading your thinking will improve your performance at school and help you feel better throughout the day whatever you're doing, whether it's playing sports, solving a problem or even just chatting! The more you use your brain, the cleverer you will become!

Kids' 10-Minute Brain Workout is a brilliant start to improving your brain, but there are also other things that you can do to help. Your brain is a part of your body so for it to be in top condition it is vital that you look after your body too:

1) Take regular physical exercise. This will get your blood pumping oxygen to your brain and you'll think more clearly.

2) Sleep well. Most people need at least eight hours sleep per night. Some need less and some need more. But if you don't get enough for you then your brain won't be able to function to its full potential.

3) Eat breakfast. A bowl of cereal or piece of toast in the morning will help your body wake up and will provide the energy your brain needs to function during the day.

4) Drink plenty of water. It's difficult to think clearly when you're dehydrated, so make sure that you keep yourself topped up with water throughout the day.

5) Eat a healthy, balanced diet. Foods that are especially good for your brain include fresh fruit and vegetables, nuts, eggs, lean meat and oily fish such as mackerel, salmon, trout and tuna (though avoid any of these foods if you are allergic to them).

As well as tackling the brain workouts in this book, you can invent your own mental challenges throughout the day. You could start from the moment you get up in the morning by eating your cereal with your other hand, and finish by learning a new word from a dictionary just before you go to sleep.

Tactical games such as chess, cards or dominoes can improve your concentration, reasoning and memory skills. Reading is very good for your brain as it helps you learn new words and phrases, improves your memory and helps you make sense of the world around you.

There are all sorts of things you can do to increase your brain powers, and you can start right now with *Kids' 10-Minute Brain Workout*.

Every workout in this book can be solved by thinking carefully about the problem in front of you. You should never need to guess in order to complete the workout. All you'll need to solve the puzzles in this book is a pencil – and your brain!

Don't be afraid to make notes or write on the pages – making notes can be a good tactic to help you keep track of your thoughts as you work on a puzzle.

Check your answers at the back of the book. If you're finding it difficult to complete an exercise, it is okay to take a quick peek at the answers. Even when you have seen the answer it can still be a challenge to work out how to get there.

Remember... you are training your brain so it's the thinking along the way that's important, not the answer itself!

To keep up with your increasing brain power, the brain workouts get steadily harder as you progress through the book. It's best to start at the beginning and work your way through, because sometimes the earlier puzzles will give you hints and tips that will help you with the later puzzles.

Are you ready to take the first step towards improving your brain power? Then turn to Brain Workout 1, and enjoy!

BRAIN
WORKOUTS

ENTER HERE

THE ANSWERS ARE AT THE BACK OF THE BOOK

BRAIN WORKOUT 1

Complete this sudoku puzzle by placing a number
from 1 to 6 in every square, but with no number
appearing more than once in each row, column
or marked two-by-three area.

	3		6	2	
		5	2	6	
			1		
		1			
	4	2	5		
	2	6		3	

BRAIN WORKOUT 2

Find the fruits in the wordsearch square below.
They might be written forwards, backwards,
up, down or diagonally.

BANANA	LIME	PEAR
BLACKBERRY	MELON	PINEAPPLE
GRAPE	NECTARINE	RASPBERRY
KIWI	ORANGE	SATSUMA
LEMON	PEACH	STRAWBERRY

Y	P	M	L	Y	R	N	N	S	N
R	R	I	M	R	E	O	A	A	E
R	M	R	N	R	M	L	K	T	C
E	R	E	E	E	C	E	I	S	T
B	B	P	L	B	A	M	W	U	A
P	E	A	R	K	W	P	I	M	R
S	R	R	N	C	E	A	P	A	I
A	E	G	N	A	R	O	R	L	N
R	M	R	C	L	N	C	R	T	E
U	R	H	L	B	P	A	A	L	S

BRAIN WORKOUT 3

An anagram is a word that can be made by rearranging the letters of another word. For example, DOG is an anagram of GOD. Unscramble the anagrams below to fill in the missing words in these sentences. Each missing word is an anagram of the word written in capital letters in the same sentence.

a) Her favourite fruits are LEMONS and _____.

b) He _____ his car to DOVER.

c) He rode a HORSE along the _____.

d) When I eat LIMES, I get a _____ on my face.

e) Take CARE when driving a _____ car.

f) ROSE thorns can make your finger _____!

g) Every time you visit ROME, you find _____ to do.

h) My uncle is a BORE who wears a purple _____.

i) At EASTER we'll drive a five-_____ car.

j) '_____ keepers,' she said to her FRIENDS.

k) The men in the MANORS were held for _____.

l) Witches have OPTIONS when mixing _____.

m) She ate it then STATED that it _____ funny!

n) Wait in the _____ for the sauce to THICKEN.

BRAIN WORKOUT 4

Find the following battleships hidden within the grids:

1 X Cruiser

2 X Destroyer

2 X Submarine

Here are some clues to help you:

- Each row and column has a number next to it indicating how many ship segments are in that row or column.
- Ships cannot be placed diagonally.
- Ships cannot touch directly to the left, right, top or bottom (though they can touch diagonally).

Puzzle A

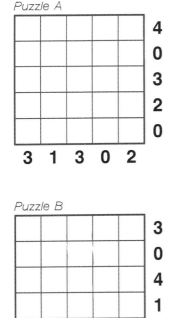

4
0
3
2
0

3 1 3 0 2

Puzzle B

3
0
4
1
1

2 3 1 0 3

BRAIN WORKOUT 5

Complete this sudoku puzzle by placing a number from 1 to 9 in every square, but with no number appearing more than once in each row, column or marked three-by-three area.

8	1		5	2			3	6
6		2	7		1	4		
9	7	3	8	6			1	
	4	9	1		5		6	
5	6		3		2		8	4
	2		9		6	5	7	
	9			5	8	6	4	3
		5	6		7	8		9
2	8			9	3		5	7

BRAIN WORKOUT 6

Fit all these animal noises into the crossword.
They can be written forwards or downwards.

BUZZ   MEOW
CHIRP   OINK
CROAK   PURR
CUCKOO   QUACK
GROWL   RIBBIT
HISS   ROAR
HOWL   SQUEAK
HUM   WOOF

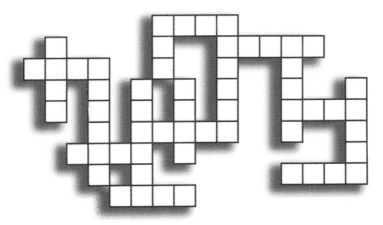

Five letters from the alphabet aren't used
in this puzzle. What are they?

BRAIN WORKOUT 7

Look at all these cartoon faces!

a) How many faces are there in total?

b) How many are either smiling or laughing?

c) How many have one eye closed and one eye open?

d) How many open eyes are there in total?

e) Without counting, work out how many closed eyes there must be.

f) How many are either wearing glasses or sticking out their tongue?

g) How many are both wearing glasses and sticking out their tongue?

BRAIN WORKOUT 8

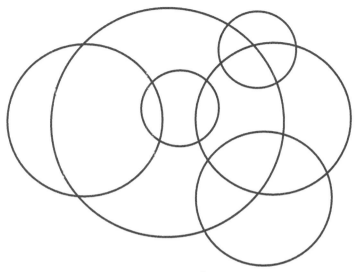

a) How many circles are there?

b) How many different sizes of circle are there?

c) How many points are there where the lines of the circles cross?

d) Where the circles overlap, new non-circular shapes are made (which do not overlap). If you wanted to colour each of these shapes a different colour, how many colours would you need?

e) What is the least number of colours you would need to colour the non-circular shapes so that no shapes of the same colour touch at any point including their corners?

BRAIN WORKOUT 9

Complete this sudoku puzzle by placing a number
from 1 to 6 in every square, but with no number
appearing more than once in each row, column
or marked two-by-three area.

				2	1
		3	6		
		4	1		
2	3				

BRAIN WORKOUT 10

Decipher this back-to-front story about computers and answer the questions below.

a) In what year was the first computer invented?

b) How much did ENIAC weigh?

c) What was the original name of Charles Babbage's computer?

d) In which country was ENIAC built?

e) What non-electrical technology did Charles Babbage's machine use?

The first computer was invented by a British man called Charles Babbage in 1822. It didn't use electricity like modern machines, but instead had a large number of mechanical cogs. He called it a 'difference engine', because it could solve complex sums. Although Babbage never finished building it, it was designed to work out tables of mathematical results. At the time, people employed to work out these tables of results were called 'computers', so the name became attached to Babbage's difference engine, and we still use the term today. The first general-purpose and fully electronic computer was built in the United States. It was called ENIAC, and was finished in 1946. It was the size of a house and weighed 30 tons. It required as much power to run as an entire town.

BRAIN WORKOUT 11

Complete these slitherlink puzzles by 'slithering' a line around each grid to link up some of the dots.

- The line must form one complete loop and use only horizontal and vertical lines to join the dots.
- The loop cannot cross or touch itself in any way.
- Each 'square' with a number in it must have precisely that many of its sides completed with a line between the dots. So a '1' has a line between the dots on one of its sides, but no lines on its other three sides.
- If there is no number in a square, it may have as many or as few sides completed as you need.

Here's a solved puzzle to help you understand:

1	3
3	1
1	3

Puzzle A

3	1	3
3		3
3	1	3

Puzzle B

1	3	2
0	3	2
1	3	2

Puzzle C

3	2	0
2		1
2	3	1

BRAIN WORKOUT 12

Complete these hashi puzzles by correctly connecting the wires to the terminals on the circuits:

- Between any pair of terminals, there can be either ONE wire, TWO wires or NO connection.
- Each terminal is numbered, telling you how many wires in total connect to it.
- All wires must connect directly vertically or horizontally, but not diagonally or with a bend.
- No two wires can cross one another.
- Wires cannot go over or under a terminal.
- The completed circuit connects in such a way that an electric current can reach every terminal by running through the wires.

Here's a solved puzzle to help you understand:

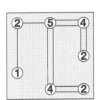

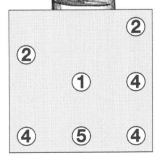

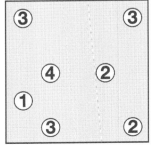

Puzzle A

Puzzle B

BRAIN WORKOUT 13

The three pieces missing from this jigsaw are mixed up with some pieces from another jigsaw. Can you find the three pieces needed to go in the gaps?

BRAIN WORKOUT 14

There are twenty-eight dominoes in a pack, each with two halves. Each half is either blank or has from one to six dots. No two dominoes are the same, and all possible combinations are found in a pack. Which three dominoes are missing from this pack?

The missing dominoes are:

BRAIN WORKOUT 15

Using just three straight lines, divide the goldfish bowl
into six areas, each area containing one
fish and one bubble.

BRAIN WORKOUT 16

Complete this sudoku puzzle by placing a number from 1 to 9 in every square, but with no number appearing more than once in each row, column or marked three-by-three area.

3	7	8		4		6	9	
6					8			7
	2	1	9				3	
8	5	6	4				2	
	3		2		1		4	
	4				7	9	8	3
	1				3	2	6	
9			6					4
	6	7		1		3	5	9

BRAIN WORKOUT 17

Shade the following squares in this grid:

- Shade squares containing even numbers. Even numbers are those in the 2-times table (2, 4, 6 and so on).
- Shade squares containing numbers that are both greater than 10 and less than 20.
- Shade squares containing numbers that are in the 3-times table (3, 6, 9 and so on).
- Shade squares containing numbers that are in the 5-times table. (Numbers in the 5 times table end in 0 or 5.)

29	1	29	7	23	31	29	1	7	18
23	53	31	43	1	53	43	23	85	13
37	41	1	37	43	49	31	20	19	65
7	29	7	23	29	1	50	5	70	95
23	2	31	49	53	23	22	27	55	23
90	24	8	53	1	84	16	17	43	49
12	15	3	18	40	15	6	47	41	37
1	30	21	15	14	4	22	37	29	7
29	7	13	14	62	9	23	31	53	23
43	23	37	25	12	7	49	29	31	1

BRAIN WORKOUT 18

These two pictures are almost identical. There are just ten differences between them - can you spot these?

BRAIN WORKOUT 19

Complete these kakuro puzzles:

- Place numbers from 1 to 9 in all the white squares.
- You must place the numbers so that each continuous run of white squares adds up to the total shown to the left or to the top of it (in the light-grey squares).
- You cannot repeat a number in any continuous run of white squares. For example, to make the total '4' you would have to use '1' and '3', since '2' and '2' would mean repeating '2'.

Puzzle A

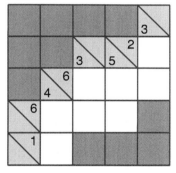

Puzzle B

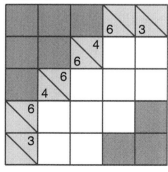

BRAIN WORKOUT 20

Find the action words in the wordsearch square below.
They might be written forwards, backwards,
up, down or diagonally.

BANG	EEYOW	POW	WHAM
BIFF	KABOOM	SMASH	WHIZ
BLAM	KACHOW	SNIKT	ZANG
BOP	KERSPLAT	THOK	ZAP
CRUNCH	KROOM	THWUNK	ZOWIE
	OOF	WAP	

Z	A	N	G	P	K	K	U	S	O	B
U	H	A	S	N	I	K	T	N	P	H
P	S	H	H	B	A	H	A	S	W	S
M	A	T	P	C	O	B	L	A	M	Y
O	M	Z	H	O	N	H	P	N	T	K
I	S	O	F	W	W	U	S	I	H	B
W	W	W	O	O	U	K	R	O	O	M
H	S	I	Y	B	M	N	E	C	K	O
A	H	E	I	O	A	Y	K	U	A	N
H	E	F	T	P	H	K	P	W	S	Y
E	F	O	I	E	W	H	I	Z	N	P

BRAIN WORKOUT 21

Complete this sudoku puzzle by placing a number
from 1 to 6 in every square, but with no number
appearing more than once in each row, column
or marked two-by-three area.

1					6
	3				4
			2	5	
	6	1			
2				1	
4					5

BRAIN WORKOUT 22

Each word ladder has a word at its top and a word at its foot. Join the bottom word to the top word by placing a new word above each step.

- Only one letter changes at each step, and it can change to any letter in the alphabet.
- Only words from the English dictionary can be used.

For example, join MAT to COT like this: MAT, CAT, COT.

BRAIN WORKOUT 23

Complete these slitherlink puzzles by 'slithering' a line around each grid to link up some of the dots.

- The line must form one complete loop and use only horizontal and vertical lines to join the dots.
- The loop cannot cross or touch itself in any way.
- Each 'square' with a number in it must have precisely that many of its sides completed with a line between the dots. So a '1' has a line between the dots on one of its sides, but no lines on its other three sides.
- If there is no number in a square, it may have as many or as few sides completed as you need.

Here's a solved puzzle to help you understand:

1	3
3	1
1	3

Puzzle A

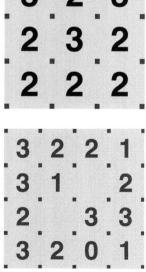

3	2	3
2	3	2
2	2	2

3	2	2	1
3	1		2
2		3	3
3	2	0	1

Puzzle B

3	2	0	0
2	2		1
3		3	3
3	1	2	2

Puzzle C

BRAIN WORKOUT 24

Spot these two pirates in the crowd.

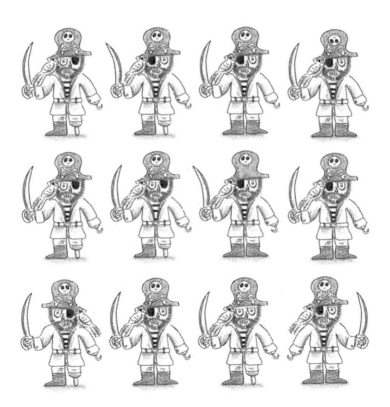

BRAIN WORKOUT 25

Complete this sudoku 'X' puzzle by placing a number
from 1 to 6 in every square, but with no number
appearing more than once in each row, column,
marked two-by-three area, or on either of the
two shaded diagonals.

3			1		
			3	6	
6		4	2		1
2		3	5		4
	4	1			
		2			6

BRAIN WORKOUT 26

Break the top-secret codes to reveal the hidden messages. Code Two is actually a hoax, designed to fool an enemy if the message is intercepted. The real message can be discovered by cracking Code Three, but you will need to crack Codes One and Two first.

CODE ONE

Each letter has been replaced by the letter that comes two before it in the alphabet. So C is written as A, D is written as B, and so on.

UCJJ BMLC ML BCAMBGLE RFGQ!

CODE TWO

Every other letter is false
(the second, fourth, sixth, etc.).

SKEMCLRIECTW MGAQP
YHZIMDSDRERNM INNM GSALRADCEIN

CODE THREE

Take the false letters from Code Two, then decipher the secret message by applying Code One.

BRAIN WORKOUT 27

Find the following battleships hidden within the grids:

1 X Cruiser

2 X Destroyer

2 X Submarine

Here are some clues to help you:

- Each row and column has a number next to it indicating how many ship segments are in that row or column.
- Ships cannot be placed diagonally.
- Ships cannot touch directly to the left, right, top or bottom (though they can touch diagonally).

Puzzle A

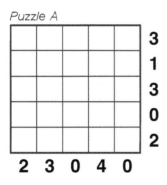

3
1
3
0
2

2 3 0 4 0

Puzzle B

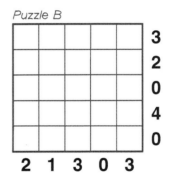

3
2
0
4
0

2 1 3 0 3

Puzzle C

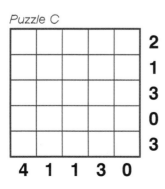

2
1
3
0
3

4 1 1 3 0

BRAIN WORKOUT 28

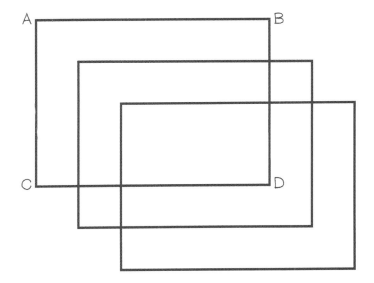

A   B

C   D

a) How many rectangles are there? (Remember that squares are rectangles too.)

b) How many points are there where the lines of the rectangles cross?

c) How many different sizes of rectangle are there?

d) Where the large rectangles overlap, new smaller shapes are made (which do not overlap). If you wanted to colour each of these new shapes a different colour, how many colours would you need?

e) If you were to draw a line from A to D and a line from B to C, how many triangles of all different sizes would there be?

BRAIN WORKOUT 29

Shade in some of the squares in these hitori puzzles so that, when each puzzle is complete, no unshaded number occurs more than once in any row or column. (This doesn't mean that every number has to occur unshaded in every row and column.)

- Shaded squares may touch diagonally but not horizontally or vertically.
- All unshaded squares must connect to each other horizontally or vertically to form a single unbroken, unshaded area.

Here's a solved puzzle to help you understand:

4	2	5	1	5
5	3	1	2	4
2	1	2	4	3
5	3	4	1	1
3	4	4	5	2

Puzzle A

2	1	3
3	3	3
3	2	1

Puzzle B

2	1	1
1	3	1
3	2	3

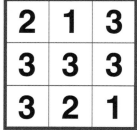

BRAIN WORKOUT 30

Complete this sudoku puzzle by placing a number
from 1 to 6 in every square, but with no number
appearing more than once in each row, column
or marked two-by-three area.

			5	6	
		4		3	1
2	4		1		
	1	2			

BRAIN WORKOUT 31

These coins are from Moneyville, where people spend quiddles (q) and quoddles (Q). There are 100 quiddles (100q) in a quoddle (1Q). There are six types of coin:

a) If you had one of each coin, how many quiddles would you have in total?

b) What is the least number of coins you would need to make up 1 quoddle without using the 1Q coin?

c) If you bought something costing 87q using a 1Q coin, what would be the least number of coins you could receive your change in?

d) You owe your friend 20 quiddles. What is the maximum number of coins you could pay him this money in if you were to give him no more than two of any coin size?

BRAIN WORKOUT 32

Using just three straight lines, divide the web into four areas, each area containing one spider and two flies.

Clue: Only one line goes right the way across the web. The other two lines go from the edge of the web to one of the other lines.

BRAIN WORKOUT 33

Normal six-sided dice have spots on each face
to represent a number from 1 to 6:

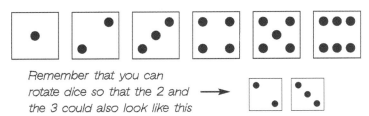

*Remember that you can
rotate dice so that the 2 and* ⟶
the 3 could also look like this

a) How many spots are there in total on all sides
of a six-sided die?

On the dice below, some spots may have rubbed off
so you can't be sure which number each face shows:

b) Which numbers could this face be?

c) What is the minimum and the maximum possible
total of these three dice?

d) What is the minimum and the maximum possible
total of these three dice?

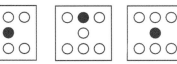

e) What possible totals could you make using these
three dice?

BRAIN WORKOUT 34

Spot these two pots of flowers in the garden.

BRAIN WORKOUT 35

Complete this sudoku 'X' puzzle by placing a number from 1 to 9 in every square, but with no number appearing more than once in each row, column, marked three-by-three area, or on either of the two shaded diagonals.

	2		7	4	6		3	9
	4	3	2					6
7	9		5	1		4	8	2
6			9	2	5		7	1
	1	7	8		4	6	2	
3	5		6	7	1			8
1	6	8		5	7		9	4
4					2	8	5	
2	3		4	8	9		6	

BRAIN WORKOUT 36

Complete each masyu puzzle by drawing a single loop that passes through the centre of every black or white circle.

- You can use only straight horizontal and vertical lines to draw the loop.
- The loop cannot enter any square more than once.
- At a BLACK circle, the loop must TURN then GO STRAIGHT on BOTH sides for at least one square.
- At a WHITE circle, the loop must GO STRAIGHT THROUGH then immediately TURN at ONE or BOTH of the squares on either side.
- In those squares that are not affected by a circle the loop can either go straight or turn.
- You do not have to use every empty square.

Puzzle A

Here's a solved puzzle to help you understand:

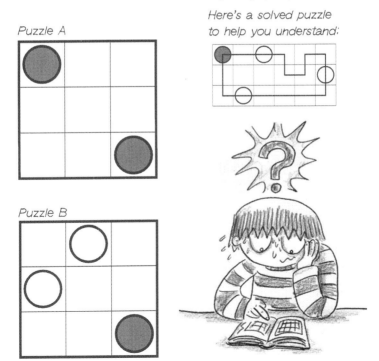

Puzzle B

BRAIN WORKOUT 37

Shade squares in these hanjie puzzles to reveal the hidden images.

The clues at the edge of each row and column reveal in order, from the left or from the top, the number of consecutive shaded squares in that row or column. For example, a clue '2, 2' would mean there are two shaded squares touching, followed by a gap of at least one empty square, and then two more shaded squares touching.

Puzzle A

```
      1 1 5 3 1
  1  [ ][ ][ ][ ][ ]
  2  [ ][ ][ ][ ][ ]
  5  [ ][ ][ ][ ][ ]
  2  [ ][ ][ ][ ][ ]
  1  [ ][ ][ ][ ][ ]
```
Puzzle A

Puzzle B

```
      1 3 5 3 1
  1  [ ][ ][ ][ ][ ]
  3  [ ][ ][ ][ ][ ]
  5  [ ][ ][ ][ ][ ]
  3  [ ][ ][ ][ ][ ]
  1  [ ][ ][ ][ ][ ]
```
Puzzle B

Puzzle C

```
        2 2 1 2 2
        2 1 1 1 2
  2, 2 [ ][ ][ ][ ][ ]
  2, 2 [ ][ ][ ][ ][ ]
    1  [ ][ ][ ][ ][ ]
  1, 1 [ ][ ][ ][ ][ ]
    5  [ ][ ][ ][ ][ ]
```
Puzzle C

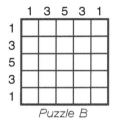

Puzzle D

```
        1 1     1 1
        1 2 3 2 1
    1  [ ][ ][ ][ ][ ]
    5  [ ][ ][ ][ ][ ]
    1  [ ][ ][ ][ ][ ]
  1, 1 [ ][ ][ ][ ][ ]
  2, 2 [ ][ ][ ][ ][ ]
```
Puzzle D

Tip: Mark squares you know must be empty with a cross, 'x'. This will help you work out where the shaded squares go!

BRAIN WORKOUT 38

Find the vehicles in the wordsearch square below.
They might be written forwards, backwards,
up, down or diagonally.

AEROPLANE   MINIBUS   TANK
AMBULANCE   MOPED   TAXI
BICYCLE   MOTORBIKE   TRACTOR
BULLDOZER   ROCKET   TRAIN
CAR   SCOOTER   TRAM
COACH   SHIP   TRUCK
LORRY   STEAMROLLER   VAN

S	H	I	P	C	M	E	T	S	I	U
O	C	S	C	O	O	T	E	R	X	C
T	B	U	A	A	P	T	C	E	A	O
R	U	B	C	C	E	R	N	L	T	M
U	L	I	Y	H	D	A	A	C	R	C
C	L	N	R	C	L	I	L	Y	O	A
K	D	I	R	P	R	N	U	C	C	A
O	O	M	O	T	O	R	B	I	K	E
Z	Z	R	L	V	A	N	M	B	E	A
R	E	L	L	O	R	M	A	E	T	S
A	R	O	T	C	A	R	T	A	N	K

BRAIN WORKOUT 39

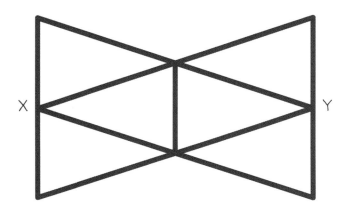

X   Y

a) How many triangles of all sizes are there?

b) How many different sizes of triangle are there?

c) What's the smallest total number of straight lines you could use to draw this diagram?

d) Is it possible to draw this diagram without taking your pen off the paper and without going over any line more than once?

e) If you drew a straight line from 'X' to 'Y', how many triangles of all sizes would there be?

BRAIN WORKOUT 40

Complete this irregular-area sudoku puzzle by placing a number from 1 to 6 in every square, but with no number appearing more than once in each row, column or marked six-square area.

2			4	5	6
3		5			2
4			2		3
6	2	4			5

BRAIN WORKOUT 41

Place eight dominoes where the double-blanks are to complete the domino chain.

- Dominoes can only touch one another when the number of spots on their touching ends match.
- You can only use the dominoes shown at the bottom of the page. You can only use each domino once.

BRAIN WORKOUT 42

Complete these kakuro puzzles:

- Place numbers from 1 to 9 in all the white squares.
- You must place the numbers so that each continuous run of white squares adds up to the total shown to the left or to the top of it (in the light-grey squares).
- You cannot repeat a number in any continuous run of white squares. For example, to make the total '4' you would have to use '1' and '3', since '2' and '2' would mean repeating '2'.

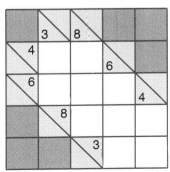

Puzzle A

Puzzle B

BRAIN WORKOUT 43

Fit all these vegetables into the crossword.
They can be written forwards or downwards.

BEANS
BEETROOT
BROCCOLI
CABBAGE
CARROT
CELERY
CORN
COURGETTE

CRESS
LEEK
ONION
POTATO
SPROUT
SWEDE
TURNIP

BRAIN WORKOUT 44

Solve these nurikabe puzzles by shading in some of their squares.

- Each number must end up as part of a separate group of that number of unshaded squares.
- Groups of unshaded squares cannot touch horizontally or vertically (though they can touch diagonally).
- Shaded squares cannot form a two-by-two block.
- All the shaded squares must connect horizontally or vertically to form a single continuous area.

CORRECT

INCORRECT

These shaded squares do not all connect vertically or horizontally and there is a shaded two-by-two block.

Puzzle A

Puzzle B

BRAIN WORKOUT 45

Complete this wordoku puzzle by placing one of the
following letters in every square, but with no letter
appearing more than once in each row, column
or marked two-by-three area:

N R K B A I

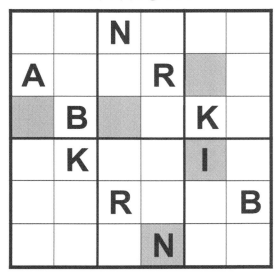

Find the hidden word by reading the letters in the
shaded squares from left to right and top to bottom.

BRAIN WORKOUT 46

The four pieces missing from this jigsaw are mixed up
with pieces from another jigsaw. Can you find the
four pieces needed to go in the gaps?

BRAIN WORKOUT 47

Each word ladder has a word at its top and a word at its foot. Join the bottom word to the top word by placing a new word above each step.

- Only one letter changes at each step, and it can change to any letter in the alphabet.
- Only words from the English dictionary can be used.

For example, join MAT to COT like this: MAT, CAT, COT.

BRAIN WORKOUT 48

Complete these slitherlink puzzles by 'slithering' a line around each grid to link up some of the dots.

- The line must form one complete loop and use only horizontal and vertical lines to join the dots.
- The loop cannot cross or touch itself in any way.
- Each 'square' with a number in it must have precisely that many of its sides completed with a line between the dots. So a '1' has a line between the dots on one of its sides, but no lines on its other three sides.
- If there is no number in a square, it may have as many or as few sides completed as you need.

Here's a solved puzzle to help you understand:

```
1     3
3     1
1     3
```

Puzzle A

```
1  0  0  0
3  2     0
1     2  1
2  1  2  3
```

```
2  1  1  2
1        2
1        3
3  3  2  3
```

```
2  2  3  3
1     2     2
1  2     1  3
3     2     3
   1  3  1  3
```

Puzzle C

BRAIN WORKOUT 49

Shade in some of the squares in these hitori puzzles so that, when each puzzle is complete, no unshaded number occurs more than once in any row or column. (This doesn't mean that every number has to occur unshaded in every row and column.)

- Shaded squares may touch diagonally but not horizontally or vertically.
- All unshaded squares must connect to each other horizontally or vertically to form a single unbroken, unshaded area.

Here's a solved puzzle to help you understand:

4	2	5	1	5
5	3	1	2	4
2	1	2	4	3
5	3	4	1	1
3	4	4	5	2

Puzzle A

3	1	2
2	3	1
2	1	1

Puzzle B

2	2	3
1	1	2
2	3	1

Puzzle C

1	1	3
3	3	2
2	3	1

BRAIN WORKOUT 50

Complete this sudoku 'X' puzzle by placing a number
from 1 to 9 in every square, but with no number
appearing more than once in each row, column,
marked three-by-three area, or on either of
the two shaded diagonals.

3		2	5	9		7		
9		8	7	2	3		4	5
	5					3		
			4		8			6
4	6		1		7		3	2
8			2		9			
		6					5	
5	9		3	8	2	1		7
		3		1	5	4		8

BRAIN WORKOUT 51

Find the following battleships hidden within the grids:

1 X Cruiser

2 X Destroyer

2 X Submarine

Here are some clues to help you:

- Each row and column has a number next to it indicating how many ship segments are in that row or column.
- Ships cannot be placed diagonally.
- Ships cannot touch directly to the left, right, top or bottom (though they can touch diagonally).

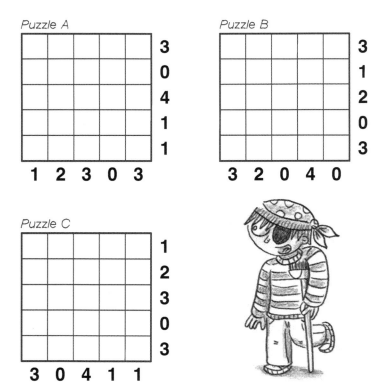

Puzzle A

3
0
4
1
1

1 2 3 0 3

Puzzle B

3
1
2
0
3

3 2 0 4 0

Puzzle C

1
2
3
0
3

3 0 4 1 1

BRAIN WORKOUT 52

a) How many stick figures have at least one arm up in the air?

b) How many have both feet facing the same way?

c) How many are both smiling and holding their arms in a U-shape that points either up or down?

d) How many have both arms pointing down and one foot up in the air?

e) How many have either their hands on their hips or are not smiling?

BRAIN WORKOUT 53

Break the top-secret codes to reveal the hidden
messages. It may help to look at things
back to front.

CODE ONE

Each vowel (A, E, I, O, U) has been replaced with the
one that comes next in the alphabet. For example,
A is written as E, E is written as I, U is written as A,
and so on.

DED YIO HAUR UBIOT THA WIIDAN CUR?
ET 'WIID' NIT GII

CODE TWO
EHT DLOG SI DEIRUB NI EHT DRAY

CODE THREE

This message has been encrypted using Code Two.
Each letter has then been replaced with the one
that comes before it in the alphabet.

MTQ QNE QTNX DEHK!

BRAIN WORKOUT 54

Complete this sudoku puzzle by placing a number
from 1 to 9 in every square, but with no number
appearing more than once in each row, column
or marked three-by-three area.

2	4					8	9	1
	6	7			3			
		9			2		3	
				3	8	1	4	
			1		9			
	8	2	4	7				
	7		6			2		
			2			3	1	
9	2	4					6	7

BRAIN WORKOUT 55

These two pictures are almost identical, with the bottom one being a mirror image of the top. However there are also ten differences between them - can you spot these?

BRAIN WORKOUT 56

Complete these hashi puzzles by correctly connecting the wires to the terminals on the circuits:

- Between any pair of terminals, there can be either ONE wire, TWO wires or NO connection.
- Each terminal is numbered, telling you how many wires in total connect to it.
- All wires must connect directly vertically or horizontally, but not diagonally or with a bend.
- No two wires can cross one another.
- Wires cannot go over or under a terminal.
- The completed circuit connects in such a way that an electric current can reach every terminal by running through the wires.

Here's a solved puzzle to help you understand:

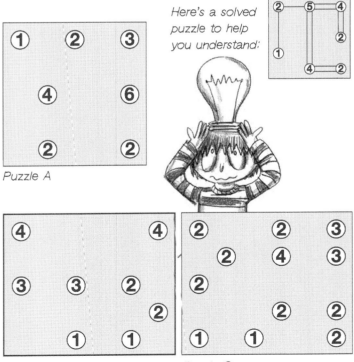

Puzzle A

Puzzle B

Puzzle C

BRAIN WORKOUT 57

Complete this irregular-area sudoku puzzle by placing a number from 1 to 6 in every square, but with no number appearing more than once in each row, column or marked six-square area.

	4	3	1		
5					1
2	3		6		
		2		3	6
1					3
		1	4	2	

BRAIN WORKOUT 58

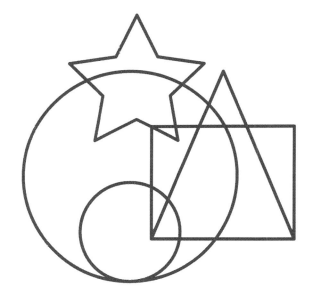

a) How many triangles are there?

b) Is it possible to draw this picture without taking your pen off the paper and without going along any line twice?

c) Where the big shapes overlap, new smaller shapes are made (which do not overlap). If you wanted to colour each of these new shapes a different colour, how many colours would you need?

d) What is the most sides that any polygon in this picture has? (A polygon is a shape made of straight lines that join up and don't cross over one another).

BRAIN WORKOUT 59

Shade the shapes correctly to reveal a picture:

- Shade shapes containing numbers that are in the 7-times table.

- Shade shapes containing numbers with the digit '2' in them (for example 2, 12, 20 etc.).

- Shade shapes containing numbers that are in both the 2-times table AND the 5-times table (for example 10 but not 2 or 5).

- Shade shapes containing numbers that are in the 3-times table (for example 3, 6, 9, 12 etc.).

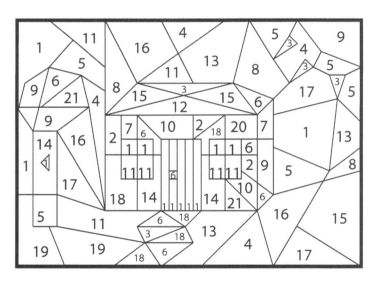

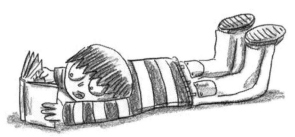

BRAIN WORKOUT 60

Complete these kakuro puzzles:
- Place numbers from 1 to 9 in all the white squares.
- You must place the numbers so that each continuous run of white squares adds up to the total shown to the left or to the top of it (in the light-grey squares).
- You cannot repeat a number in any continuous run of white squares. For example, to make the total '4' you would have to use '1' and '3', since '2' and '2' would mean repeating '2'.

Puzzle A

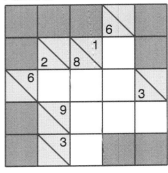

Puzzle B

BRAIN WORKOUT 61

Find 'thank you' in many languages in the wordsearch square below. The words might be written forwards, backwards, up, down or diagonally.

ARIGATO (Japanese)

DANKE (German)

DEKUJI (Czech)

DOH JE (Cantonese)

DZIEKUJE (Polish)

EFHARISTO (Greek)

GRACIAS (Spanish)

GRAZIE (Italian)

KIITOS (Finnish)

MERCI (French)

OBRIGADO (Portuguese)

SPASIBO (Russian)

TACK (Swedish)

TAKK (Norwegian)

TERIMA KASIH (Indonesian)

TODA (Hebrew)

(You're not looking for the names of the languages.)

O	R	O	A	H	A	F	O	O	S	E
A	D	O	T	I	C	S	I	S	U	I
R	I	A	T	S	P	T	A	I	E	O
I	T	E	N	A	I	I	C	J	O	U
G	B	R	S	K	C	R	U	D	K	I
A	T	I	K	A	E	K	A	A	I	J
T	B	A	R	M	E	G	I	H	O	U
O	T	G	K	I	I	T	O	S	F	K
Z	G	D	Z	R	R	D	O	H	J	E
Z	A	D	B	E	I	Z	A	R	G	D
S	R	O	A	T	T	J	T	H	E	P

BRAIN WORKOUT 62

Complete this wordoku puzzle by placing one of the
following letters in every square, but with no letter
appearing more than once in each row, column
or marked two-by-three area:

Z P L E S U

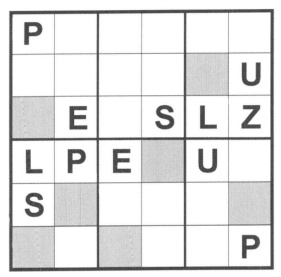

Find the hidden word by reading the letters in the
shaded squares from left to right and top to bottom.

BRAIN WORKOUT 63

These banknotes are from Moneyville, where people count their fortunes in quidillions (Qd). There are six types of banknote:

a) If you had one of each banknote, how many quidillions would you have?

b) If you bought something that cost 95Qd by giving the exact amount of money, what is the least number of banknotes that you could use to pay for it?

c) I have two of each banknote. How many banknotes will I have left if I buy something that costs 1365Qd?

d) If you only use the banknotes with numbers that start with '5', what is the least number of banknotes you can use to buy something that costs 1105Qd?

BRAIN WORKOUT 64

Complete each masyu puzzle by drawing a single
loop that passes through the centre of every black
or white circle.

- You can use only straight horizontal and vertical
  lines to draw the loop.
- The loop cannot enter any square more than once.
- At a BLACK circle, the loop must TURN then GO
  STRAIGHT on BOTH sides for at least one square.
- At a WHITE circle, the loop must GO STRAIGHT
  THROUGH then immediately TURN at ONE or
  BOTH of the squares on either side.
- In those squares that are not affected by a circle
  the loop can either go straight or turn.
- You do not have to use every empty square.

Puzzle A

*Here's a solved puzzle
to help you understand:*

Puzzle B

BRAIN WORKOUT 65

Spot these two monsters in the crowd.

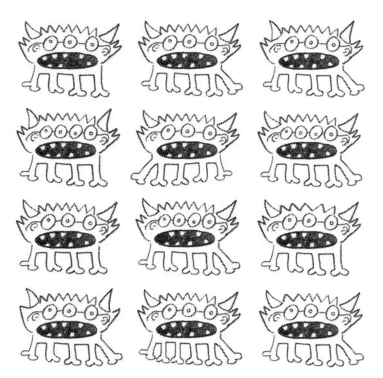

BRAIN WORKOUT 66

Solve these nurikabe puzzles by shading in some of their squares.

- Each number must end up as part of a separate group of that number of unshaded squares.
- Groups of unshaded squares cannot touch horizontally or vertically (though they can touch diagonally).
- Shaded squares cannot form a two-by-two block.
- All the shaded squares must connect horizontally or vertically to form a single continuous area.

CORRECT

INCORRECT

These shaded squares do not all connect vertically or horizontally and there is a shaded two-by-two block.

Puzzle A

Puzzle B

BRAIN WORKOUT 67

Complete this sudoku puzzle by placing a number
from 1 to 9 in every square, but with no number
appearing more than once in each row, column
or marked three-by-three area.

1		5			6	3		
	3						6	
	9	6	3	7				5
	6	4	2	5				
	7						5	
				8	3	4	2	
3				4	7	2	9	
	4						8	
		1	8			6		7

BRAIN WORKOUT 68

An anagram is a word that can be made by rearranging the letters of another word.
For example, DOG is an anagram of GOD.

Unscramble the anagrams below to fill in the missing words in these sentences. Each missing word is an anagram of the word written in capital letters in the same sentence.

a) 'I like your coloured MARKERS,' _____ Sam.

b) He SECURED the boat and _____ the people.

c) Display NOTICES in this _____ of the shop.

d) You need good _____ to run on all TERRAINS.

e) NAMELESS _____ are forever telephoning me.

f) I have a _____ who is ORIENTAL.

g) He TRIED hard to run, but he was too _____.

h) She SAVES her money to buy ceramic _____.

i) If you want to LISTEN it helps if you are _____.

j) The _____ caught the CHEATER.

k) On _____ we learnt about the DYNAMO.

l) Everyone AGREES that _____ is messy.

m) Which creepy-crawly is the NICEST _____?

n) He saw a scary THING in the dark that _____.

BRAIN WORKOUT 69

Using just four straight lines, divide the window into six areas, each area containing one rocket, one flying saucer and one star.

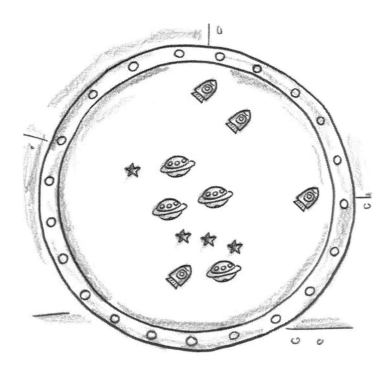

Clue: None of the lines go all the way from one side of the window to the other. They all run only from the edge of the circle to one of the other lines.

BRAIN WORKOUT 70

Complete this irregular-area sudoku puzzle by placing
a number from 1 to 9 in every square, but with no
number appearing more than once in each row,
column or marked nine-square area.

9			1		3	4	6	
		6	5	4	9	2		8
	7				8			9
	1			6		3		2
6		4				1		7
3		1		2			5	
8			7				4	
2		3	4	8	1	7		
	4	7	6		5			3

BRAIN WORKOUT 71

Complete this hashi puzzle by correctly connecting the wires to the terminals on the circuit:

- Between any pair of terminals, there can be either ONE wire, TWO wires or NO connection.
- Each terminal is numbered, telling you how many wires in total connect to it.
- All wires must connect directly vertically or horizontally, but not diagonally or with a bend.
- No two wires can cross one another.
- Wires cannot go over or under a terminal.
- The completed circuit connects in such a way that an electric current can reach every terminal by running through the wires.

Here's a solved puzzle to help you understand:

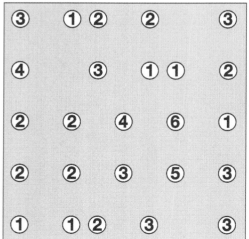

BRAIN WORKOUT 72

Break the top-secret codes to reveal the
hidden messages.

CODE ONE
Each pair of letters has been swapped, for example
ABCDEFGH is written BADCFEHG.

ATEKISSXETSPAETSNAFDUOSRE
TSPONTRH

CODE TWO
Each letter has been replaced by a number
representing its position in the alphabet: A=1,
B=2, and so on up to Z=26.

20 8 9 19 9 19 3 15 18 18 5 3 20

CODE THREE
This message has been encrypted using Code Two
from brain workout 26, then Code One from Brain
Workout 53. It has then been flipped so that the
whole message is back to front.

RNAOKTUTAHRIBSABDIITCORFATTHSEU
MMEUSASRAUGOEIOYK

BRAIN WORKOUT 73

Find the following battleships hidden within the grid:

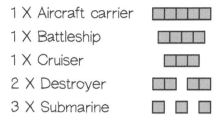

1 X Aircraft carrier

1 X Battleship

1 X Cruiser

2 X Destroyer

3 X Submarine

Here are some clues to help you:

- Each row and column has a number next to it indicating how many ship segments are in that row or column.

- Ships cannot be placed diagonally.

- Ships cannot touch directly to the left, right, top or bottom (though they can touch diagonally).

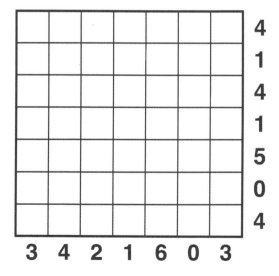

BRAIN WORKOUT 74

Complete this sudoku puzzle by placing a number
from 1 to 9 in every square, but with no number
appearing more than once in each row, column
or marked three-by-three area.

4	1		7					
			4	1				9
8		7	9		2			3
		4				2	6	1
	9						7	
6	2	8				5		
7			2		9	1		5
1				6	5			
					1		2	6

BRAIN WORKOUT 75

These two pictures are almost identical, with the bottom one being an upside-down image of the top. There are ten differences between them - can you spot these?

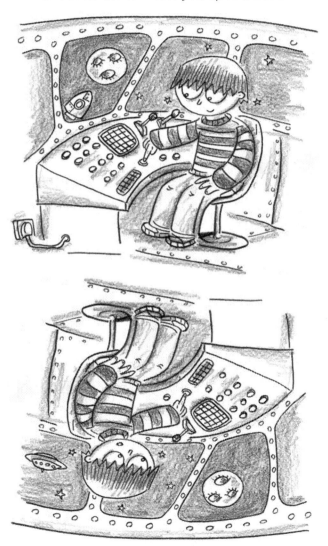

BRAIN WORKOUT 76

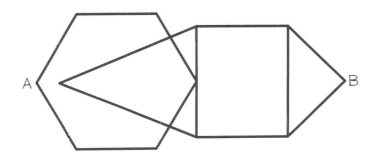

a) How many triangles are there?

b) How many quadrilaterals are there? (Quadrilaterals are shapes with four sides. The sides do not all have to be the same length.)

c) How many hexagons are there? (Hexagons are shapes with six sides. The sides do not all have to be the same length.)

d) Where the large shapes overlap, new smaller shapes are made (which do not overlap). If you wanted to colour each of these new shapes a different colour, how many colours would you need?

e) If you were to draw a line from A to B how many triangles would there then be?

BRAIN WORKOUT 77

Complete these kakuro puzzles:

- Place numbers from 1 to 9 in all the white squares.
- You must place the numbers so that each continuous run of white squares adds up to the total shown to the left or to the top of it (in the light-grey squares).
- You cannot repeat a number in any continuous run of white squares. For example, to make the total '4' you would have to use '1' and '3', since '2' and '2' would mean repeating '2'.

Puzzle A

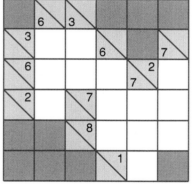

Puzzle B

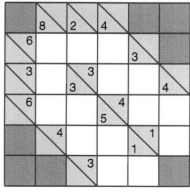

BRAIN WORKOUT 78

Decipher this muddled, back-to-front story about cinema and answer the questions below. Watch out, each pair of lines has been swapped, so that the second line comes before the first.

a) In what decade was photography introduced?

b) When were the first films with sound released?

c) What was the name of the first public system for playing back films?

d) What was the name of the brothers who demonstrated the first projector system? And when did they first reveal it?

photography in the 1830s,
Following the introduction of
playing a series of photographs
systems were developed for
the illusion that the picture was
in quick succession. This gave
in this way today. The first
moving, and cinema still works
reel of film with many pictures
public system to play back a
called the Kinetoscope, but it
on was revealed in 1893. It was
one person could watch the
was not very popular as only
the Lumière brothers
film at a time. In 1895, however,
Cinématographe projector
demonstrated their
cinema was born. Due to the
system in France, and modern
films were only a minute long.
lengths of film required, early
they were in black and white.
There was also no sound and
mainstream films in 1926, and in
Sound was first added to
produced. At this point colour
1934 the first colour films were
to make, and it was many
films were very expensive
widely available.
years before they were

BRAIN WORKOUT 79

Shade in some of the squares in these hitori puzzles so that, when each puzzle is complete, no unshaded number occurs more than once in any row or column. (This doesn't mean that every number has to occur unshaded in every row and column.)

- Shaded squares may touch diagonally but not horizontally or vertically.
- All unshaded squares must connect to each other horizontally or vertically to form a single unbroken, unshaded area.

Here's a solved puzzle to help you understand:

4	2	5	1	5
5	3	1	2	4
2	1	2	4	3
5	3	4	1	1
3	4	4	5	2

Puzzle A

2	3	3	4
1	1	2	3
3	2	3	1
4	1	4	2

Puzzle B

4	3	2	1
1	1	4	2
2	4	3	4
1	4	2	2

BRAIN WORKOUT 80

Complete this sudoku puzzle by placing a number from 1 to 9 in every square, but with no number appearing more than once in each row, column or marked three-by-three area.

		9	1		4	2	6	
		3		8	5			
		4	2	6				
	2	6		5				
	3		4		8		2	
				2		7	5	
				1	9	3		
			6	4		8		
	5	2	8		3	1		

BRAIN WORKOUT 81

Complete these slitherlink puzzles by 'slithering' a line around each grid to link up some of the dots.

- The line must form one complete loop and use only horizontal and vertical lines to join the dots.
- The loop cannot cross or touch itself in any way.
- Each 'square' with a number in it must have precisely that many of its sides completed with a line between the dots. So a '1' has a line between the dots on one of its sides, but no lines on its other three sides.
- If there is no number in a square, it may have as many or as few sides completed as you need.

Here's a solved puzzle to help you understand:

1		3
3		1
1		3

Puzzle A

2	1	1	3
1			3
1			2
2	2	3	3

3	2	2	3	3	3
3	2		1	2	1
3	1	1	1		3
2		2	1	1	2
3	2	3		3	3
2	2	2	1	2	2

Puzzle B

BRAIN WORKOUT 82

Find the cloud types below in the wordsearch square.
They might be written forwards, backwards,
up, down or diagonally.

ALTOCUMULUS
ALTOSTRATUS
CIRROCUMULUS
CIRROSTRATUS

CIRRUS
CUMULONIMBUS
NIMBOSTRATUS
STRATOCUMULUS

S	S	U	B	M	I	N	O	L	U	M	U	C	C
C	U	U	L	S	S	S	U	U	O	U	O	T	R
L	S	U	T	A	R	T	S	O	B	M	I	N	T
N	U	S	M	A	S	R	M	U	S	M	U	R	T
O	T	S	O	L	R	A	I	C	L	U	O	L	S
T	A	U	T	T	T	T	R	T	C	B	A	T	M
T	R	S	A	O	C	O	S	S	M	S	T	U	T
L	T	R	T	C	O	C	M	O	M	U	M	O	S
U	S	U	L	U	M	U	C	O	R	R	I	C	L
R	O	A	I	M	T	M	C	L	C	R	R	T	U
O	T	N	L	U	B	U	L	N	M	I	I	O	M
T	L	R	U	L	M	L	I	S	L	C	O	C	T
B	A	I	L	U	T	U	A	L	C	M	C	U	U
O	S	I	S	S	I	S	U	U	L	L	C	U	U

BRAIN WORKOUT 83

Shade squares in these hanjie puzzles to reveal the hidden images.

The clues at the edge of each row and column reveal in order, from the left or from the top, the number of consecutive shaded squares in that row or column. For example, a clue '2, 2' would mean there are two shaded squares touching, followed by a gap of at least one empty square, and then two more shaded squares touching.

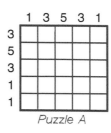

Puzzle A

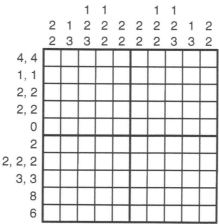

Puzzle B

Tip: Mark squares you know must be empty with a cross, 'x'. This will help you work out where the shaded squares go!

BRAIN WORKOUT 84

Break the top-secret codes to reveal the hidden messages. When you've cracked Code Two, you will reveal a question that can be answered by cracking Code Three.

CODE ONE

Letters in this message have been coded to give numbers that represent their positions in the alphabet: A=1, B=2, and so on up to Z=26. However, these code numbers are not visible. Instead, the 'hidden' code numbers are the differences between the consecutive visible numbers. For example, the numbers '05 13' have a difference of 8 between them, and the eighth letter in the alphabet is 'H', so '05 13' is the code for 'H', and '05 13 04' is the code for 'HI'.

06 29 24 36 24 20 35 21 16

CODE TWO

This message has been coded so that every other letter, including the '?', is false (the first, third, fifth, etc.) These false letters, when read backwards, complete the message.

?WEHZYIDRIPDLTEHBEOCNOEWHWTIN

CODE THREE

Each pair of letters, including the '!', has been swapped around. For example ABCD is written BADC.

EBACSUI EW TSA UOSTATDNNII
GI NST IFLE!D

BRAIN WORKOUT 85

Complete this irregular-area sudoku puzzle by placing
a number from 1 to 9 in every square, but with no
number appearing more than once in each row,
column or marked nine-square area.

5	3	2	9					1
	6	4	7		9	3	5	
					8		6	3
4						2		
6	4	9	1		2	5	3	7
		1						5
2	9		8					
	2	8	3		6	1	7	
1					3	8	2	9

BRAIN WORKOUT 86

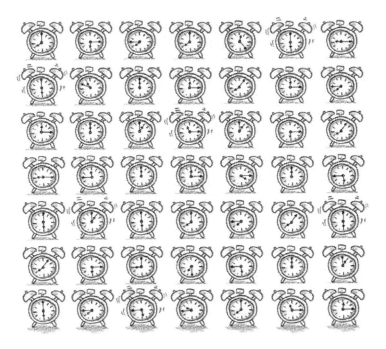

a) How many clocks are there?

b) How many are ringing?

c) How many show 15 minutes past the hour?

d) How many show 'quarter to' or 'o'clock'?

e) How many are showing either 11:15 or 8:05?

f) How many different times are there in total?

BRAIN WORKOUT 87

Normal six-sided dice have spots on each side to represent a number from 1 to 6:

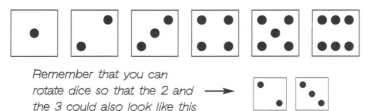

Remember that you can rotate dice so that the 2 and the 3 could also look like this ⟶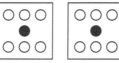

a) If you roll two six-sided dice one after the other, how many ways can you get a total of seven?

On the dice below, some spots have rubbed off so you can't be sure which number each die is showing:

b) What is the minimum and the maximum possible total of these two dice?

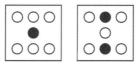

c) What is the minimum and the maximum possible total of these two dice?

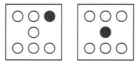

d) What different totals can you make with these two dice?

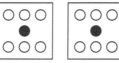

e) Using the same two dice as in (d), how many different doubles can you make? (A double is when you have two dice of the same value).

BRAIN WORKOUT 88

Each word ladder has a word at its top and a word at its foot. Join the bottom word to the top word by placing a new word above each step.

- Only one letter changes at each step, and it can change to any letter in the alphabet.
- Only words from the English dictionary can be used.

For example, join MAT to COT like this: MAT, CAT, COT.

CAT

DOG

HIDE

FIND

LOOK

pigeon

moo

oink

SEES

This ladder contains clues to some of its steps.

BRAIN WORKOUT 89

Using just four straight lines, divide the field into
five areas, each area containing one tree,
one bush and one sheep.

*Clue: Only one of the lines goes all the way from one side of
the field to the other. The other three lines run only from the
edge of the field to one of the other lines.*

BRAIN WORKOUT 90

Complete this sudoku puzzle by placing a number
from 1 to 9 in every square, but with no number
appearing more tnan once in each row, column
or markea three-by-three area.

3	9				6		4	1
				5				
7			1				5	2
2	6		8	7				
9				4				6
				9	1		3	4
4	7				8			9
				2				
8	1		7				2	3

THE
ANSWERS

BRAIN WORKOUT 1
ANSWERS

5	3	4	6	2	1
4	1	5	2	6	3
2	6	3	1	5	4
6	5	1	3	4	2
3	4	2	5	1	6
1	2	6	4	3	5

BRAIN WORKOUT 2
ANSWERS

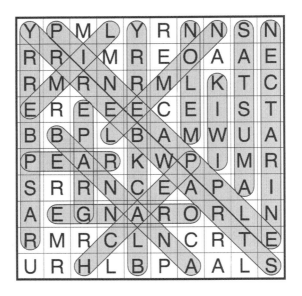

BRAIN WORKOUT 3
ANSWERS

a) Her favourite fruits are LEMONS and MELONS.

b) He DROVE his car to DOVER.

c) He rode a HORSE along the SHORE.

d) When I eat LIMES, I get a SMILE on my face.

e) Take CARE when driving a RACE car.

f) ROSE thorns can make your finger SORE!

g) Every time you visit ROME, you find MORE to do.

h) My uncle is a BORE who wears a purple ROBE.

i) At EASTER we'll drive a five-SEATER car.

j) 'FINDERS keepers,' she said to her FRIENDS.

k) The men in the MANORS were held for RANSOM.

l) Witches have OPTIONS when mixing POTIONS.

m) She ate it then STATED that it TASTED funny!

n) Wait in the KITCHEN for the sauce to THICKEN.

BRAIN WORKOUT 4
ANSWERS

Puzzle A

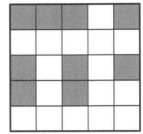

Puzzle B

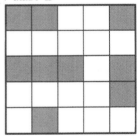

BRAIN WORKOUT 5
ANSWERS

8	1	4	5	2	9	7	3	6
6	5	2	7	3	1	4	9	8
9	7	3	8	6	4	2	1	5
7	4	9	1	8	5	3	6	2
5	6	1	3	7	2	9	8	4
3	2	8	9	4	6	5	7	1
1	9	7	2	5	8	6	4	3
4	3	5	6	1	7	8	2	9
2	8	6	4	9	3	1	5	7

BRAIN WORKOUT 6
ANSWERS

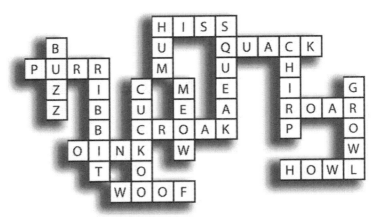

The five letters from the alphabet that aren't used
in this puzzle are D, J, V, X and Y.

BRAIN WORKOUT 7
ANSWERS

a) 49 faces

b) 27 faces

c) 12 faces

d) 66 eyes

e) 32 eyes
(49 faces each with
2 eyes, minus 66 eyes)

f) 11 faces

g) 0 faces

BRAIN WORKOUT 8
ANSWERS

a) 6 circles
b) 4 different sizes
c) 16 points
d) 17 colours
e) 4 colours

BRAIN WORKOUT 9
ANSWERS

5	4	1	2	6	3
3	6	5	4	2	1
1	2	3	6	4	5
6	5	4	1	3	2
2	3	6	5	1	4
4	1	2	3	5	6

BRAIN WORKOUT 10
ANSWERS

a) The first computer was invented in 1822.

b) ENIAC weighed 30 tons.

c) Charles Babbage originally called his computer a 'difference engine'.

d) ENIAC was built in the United States.

e) Babbage's machine used mechanical cogs.

BRAIN WORKOUT 11
ANSWERS

Puzzle A

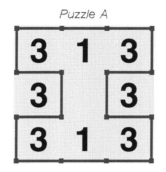

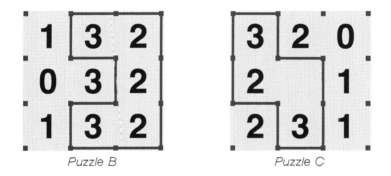

Puzzle B   *Puzzle C*

BRAIN WORKOUT 12
ANSWERS

Puzzle A

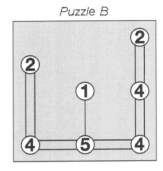

Puzzle B

BRAIN WORKOUT 13
ANSWERS

BRAIN WORKOUT 14
ANSWERS

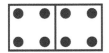

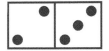

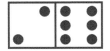

BRAIN WORKOUT 15
ANSWERS

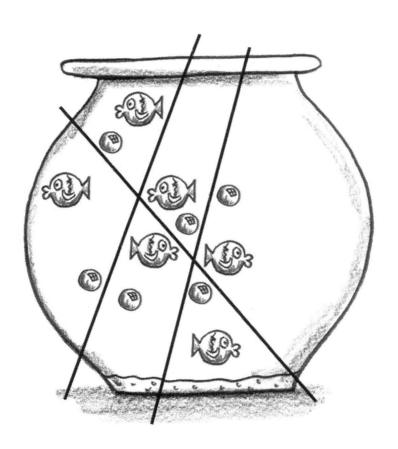

BRAIN WORKOUT 16
ANSWERS

3	7	8	1	4	5	6	9	2
6	9	5	3	2	8	4	1	7
4	2	1	9	7	6	8	3	5
8	5	6	4	3	9	7	2	1
7	3	9	2	8	1	5	4	6
1	4	2	5	6	7	9	8	3
5	1	4	7	9	3	2	6	8
9	8	3	6	5	2	1	7	4
2	6	7	8	1	4	3	5	9

BRAIN WORKOUT 17
ANSWERS

29	1	29	7	23	31	29	1	7	18
23	53	31	43	1	53	43	23	85	13
37	41	1	37	43	49	31	20	19	65
7	29	7	23	29	1	50	5	70	95
23	2	31	49	53	23	22	27	55	23
90	24	8	53	1	84	16	17	43	49
12	15	3	18	40	15	6	47	41	37
1	30	21	15	14	4	22	37	29	7
29	7	13	14	62	9	23	31	53	23
43	23	37	25	12	7	49	29	31	1

BRAIN WORKOUT 18
ANSWERS

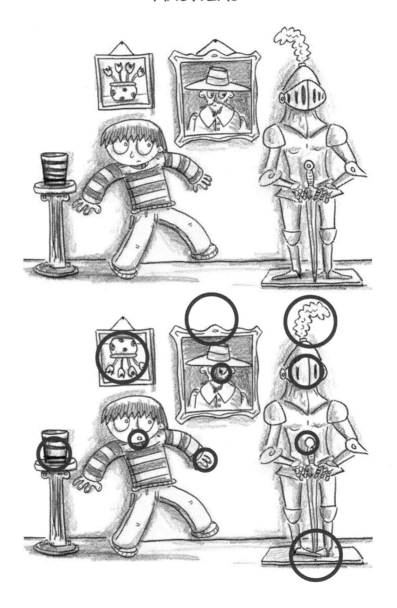

BRAIN WORKOUT 19
ANSWERS

Puzzle A

				3
		3	5 / 2	**2**
	4 / 6	**2**	**3**	**1**
6	**3**	**1**	**2**	
1	**1**			

Puzzle B

			6	3
		6 / 4	**3**	**1**
	4 / 6	**3**	**1**	**2**
6	**3**	**1**	**2**	
3	**1**	**2**		

BRAIN WORKOUT 20
ANSWERS

BRAIN WORKOUT 21
ANSWERS

1	2	5	4	3	6
5	3	6	1	2	4
6	4	3	2	5	1
3	6	1	5	4	2
2	5	4	6	1	3
4	1	2	3	6	5

BRAIN WORKOUT 22
ANSWERS

MOO

BOO

BOA

BAA

BOY

BAY

BAN

MAN

BUS

BUT

CUT

CAT

CAR

Can you find any alternative solutions?

BRAIN WORKOUT 23
ANSWERS

Puzzle A

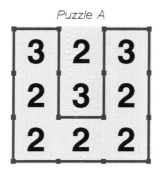

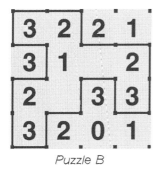

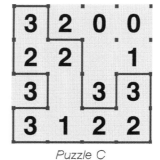

Puzzle B   *Puzzle C*

BRAIN WORKOUT 24
ANSWERS

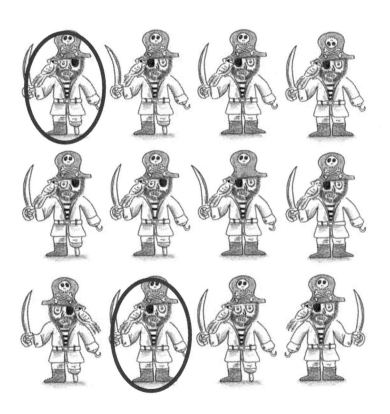

BRAIN WORKOUT 25
ANSWERS

3	2	6	1	4	5
4	1	5	3	6	2
6	5	4	2	3	1
2	6	3	5	1	4
5	4	1	6	2	3
1	3	2	4	5	6

BRAIN WORKOUT 26
ANSWERS

CODE ONE

WELL DONE ON DECODING THIS!

CODE TWO

SECRET MAP HIDDEN IN GARDEN

CODE THREE

MONKEY IS ABOUT TO POUNCE!

BRAIN WORKOUT 27
ANSWERS

Puzzle A

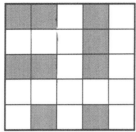

Puzzle B

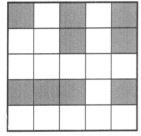

Puzzle C

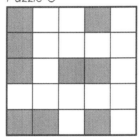

BRAIN WORKOUT 28
ANSWERS

a) 8 rectangles
b) 6 points
c) 4 different sizes
d) 7 colours
e) 15 triangles

BRAIN WORKOUT 29
ANSWERS

Puzzle A

2	1	3
3	3	3
3	2	1

Puzzle B

2	1	1
1	3	1
3	2	3

BRAIN WORKOUT 30
ANSWERS

4	3	1	6	2	5
1	2	3	5	6	4
6	5	4	2	3	1
2	4	6	1	5	3
5	1	2	3	4	6
3	6	5	4	1	2

BRAIN WORKOUT 31
ANSWERS

A) 168 quiddles
   (100q + 50q + 10q + 5q + 2q + 1q)
B) 2 coins (50q + 50q)
C) 3 coins (10q + 2q + 1q)
D) 5 coins (10q + 5q + 2q + 2q + 1q)

BRAIN WORKOUT 32
ANSWERS

BRAIN WORKOUT 33
ANSWERS

a) 21 spots

b) 2, 3, 4, 5, 6

c) The minumum total is 5
The maximum total is 17

d) The minumum total is 7
The maximum total is 15

e) 10, 12, 14, 16

BRAIN WORKOUT 35
ANSWERS

8	2	1	7	4	6	5	3	9
5	4	3	2	9	8	7	1	6
7	9	6	5	1	3	4	8	2
6	8	4	9	2	5	3	7	1
9	1	7	8	3	4	6	2	5
3	5	2	6	7	1	9	4	8
1	6	8	3	5	7	2	9	4
4	7	9	1	6	2	8	5	3
2	3	5	4	8	9	1	6	7

BRAIN WORKOUT 36
ANSWERS

Puzzle A

Puzzle B

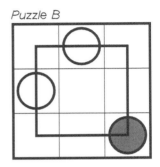

BRAIN WORKOUT 37
ANSWERS

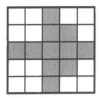

Puzzle A

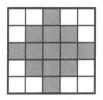

Puzzle B

Puzzle C

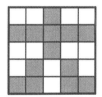

Puzzle D

BRAIN WORKOUT 38
ANSWERS

BRAIN WORKOUT 39
ANSWERS

a) 8 triangles
b) 2 sizes
c) 7 straight lines
d) Yes
e) 18 triangles

BRAIN WORKOUT 40
ANSWERS

2	1	3	4	5	6
3	6	5	1	4	2
5	4	2	6	3	1
1	3	6	5	2	4
4	5	1	2	6	3
6	2	4	3	1	5

BRAIN WORKOUT 41
ANSWERS

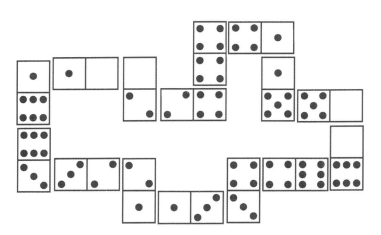

BRAIN WORKOUT 42
ANSWERS

Puzzle A

		9		
	3	**3**	6	1
	7 / 3	**4**	**2**	**1**
6	**3**	**2**	**1**	
		3	**3**	

Puzzle B

	3	8		
4	**1**	**3**	6	
6	**2**	**1**	**3**	4
	8	**4**	**1**	**3**
		3	**2**	**1**

BRAIN WORKOUT 43
ANSWERS

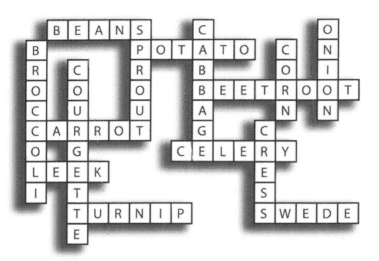

BRAIN WORKOUT 44
ANSWERS

Puzzle A

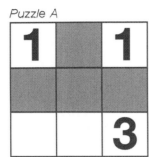

Puzzle B

BRAIN WORKOUT 45
ANSWERS

K	I	N	B	R	A
A	N	K	R	B	I
R	B	A	I	K	I
N	K	B	A	I	R
K	A	R	K	N	B
B	R	I	N	A	K

The hidden word is BRAIN.

BRAIN WORKOUT 46
ANSWERS

BRAIN WORKOUT 47
ANSWERS

HEAD
BEAD
BEND
BAND

GOLD
COLD
CORD
CORN
COIN

ROAD
LOAD
LORD
LARD
LAND
LANE

Can you find any alternative solutions?

BRAIN WORKOUT 48
ANSWERS

Puzzle A

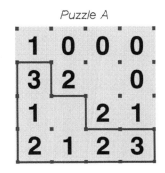

Puzzle B

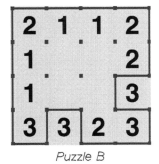

Puzzle C

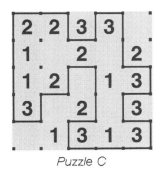

BRAIN WORKOUT 49
ANSWERS

Puzzle A

3	1	2
2	3	1
2	1	1

Puzzle B

2	2	3
1	1	2
2	3	1

Puzzle C

1	1	3
3	3	2
2	3	1

BRAIN WORKOUT 50
ANSWERS

3	4	2	5	9	6	7	8	1
9	1	8	7	2	3	6	4	5
6	5	7	8	4	1	3	2	9
2	7	5	4	3	8	9	1	6
4	6	9	1	5	7	8	3	2
8	3	1	2	6	9	5	7	4
1	8	6	9	7	4	2	5	3
5	9	4	3	8	2	1	6	7
7	2	3	6	1	5	4	9	8

BRAIN WORKOUT 51
ANSWERS

Puzzle A

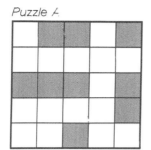

Puzzle B

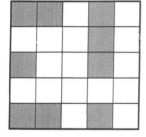

Puzzle C

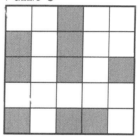

BRAIN WORKOUT 52
ANSWERS

a) 12 stick figures
b) 18 stick figures
c) 6 stick figures
d) 4 stick figures
e) 16 stick figures

BRAIN WORKOUT 53
ANSWERS

CODE ONE
DID YOU HEAR ABOUT THE
WOODEN CAR?

IT 'WOOD' NOT GO!

CODE TWO
THE GOLD IS BURIED IN THE YARD

CODE THREE
RUN FOR YOUR LIFE!

BRAIN WORKOUT 54
ANSWERS

2	4	3	7	6	5	8	9	1
8	6	7	9	1	3	4	2	5
5	1	9	8	4	2	7	3	6
7	9	6	5	3	8	1	4	2
4	3	5	1	2	9	6	7	8
1	8	2	4	7	6	9	5	3
3	7	1	6	5	4	2	8	9
6	5	8	2	9	7	3	1	4
9	2	4	3	8	1	5	6	7

BRAIN WORKOUT 55
ANSWERS

BRAIN WORKOUT 56
ANSWERS

Puzzle A

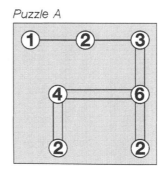

Puzzle B

Puzzle C

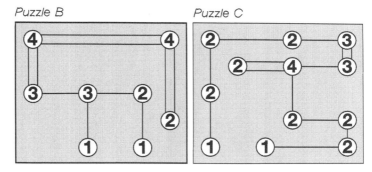

BRAIN WORKOUT 57
ANSWERS

6	4	3	1	5	2
5	2	6	3	4	1
2	3	5	6	1	4
4	1	2	5	3	6
1	5	4	2	6	3
3	6	1	4	2	5

BRAIN WORKOUT 58
ANSWERS

a) 5 triangles
b) Yes
c) 15 colours
d) 17 sides

BRAIN WORKOUT 59
ANSWERS

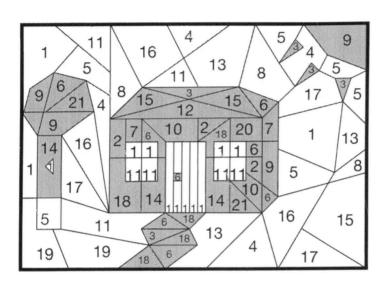

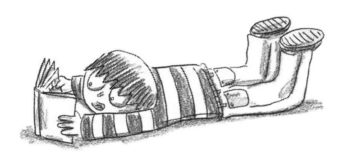

BRAIN WORKOUT 60
ANSWERS

Puzzle A

	3	6		4
4	**3**	**1**	6 / 1	**1**
7 / 6	**2**	**1**		**3**
9	**4**	**3**	**2**	2
3	**3**	5	**3**	**2**

Puzzle B

			6	
	2	8 / 1	**1**	
6	**2**	**1**	**3**	3
	9	**4**	**2**	**3**
	3	**3**		

BRAIN WORKOUT 61
ANSWERS

O	R	O	A	H	A	F	O	O	S	E
A	D	O	T	I	C	S	I	S	U	I
R	I	A	T	S	P	T	A	I	E	O
I	T	E	N	A	I	I	C	J	O	U
G	B	R	S	K	C	R	U	D	K	I
A	T	I	K	A	E	K	A	A	I	J
T	B	A	R	M	E	G	I	H	O	U
O	T	G	K	I	I	T	O	S	F	K
Z	G	D	Z	R	R	D	O	H	J	E
Z	A	D	B	E	I	Z	A	R	G	D
S	R	O	A	T	T	J	T	H	E	P

BRAIN WORKOUT 62
ANSWERS

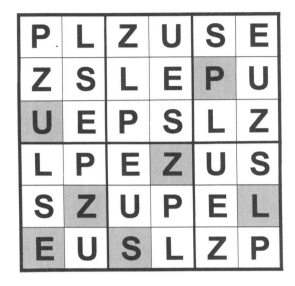

P	L	Z	U	S	E
Z	S	L	E	P	U
U	E	P	S	L	Z
L	P	E	Z	U	S
S	Z	U	P	E	L
E	U	S	L	Z	P

The hidden word is PUZZLES.

BRAIN WORKOUT 63
ANSWERS

a) 685Qd

b) 4 banknotes
   (50Qd + 20Qd + 20Qd + 5Qd)

c) 1 banknote (5Qd)

d) 5 banknotes
   (500Qd + 500Qd + 50Qd + 50Qd + 5Qd

BRAIN WORKOUT 64
ANSWERS

Puzzle A

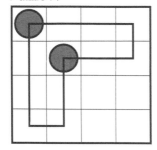

Puzzle B

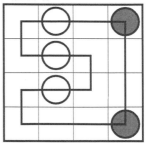

BRAIN WORKOUT 65
ANSWERS

BRAIN WORKOUT 66
ANSWERS

Puzzle A

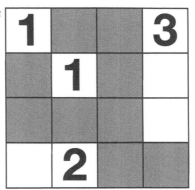

Puzzle B

BRAIN WORKOUT 67
ANSWERS

1	8	5	4	9	6	3	7	2
7	3	2	5	1	8	9	6	4
4	9	6	3	7	2	8	1	5
8	6	4	2	5	1	7	3	9
2	7	3	9	6	4	1	5	8
5	1	9	7	8	3	4	2	6
3	5	8	6	4	7	2	9	1
6	4	7	1	2	9	5	8	3
9	2	1	8	3	5	6	4	7

BRAIN WORKOUT 68
ANSWERS

a) 'I like your coloured MARKERS,' REMARKS Sam.

b) He SECURED the boat and RESCUED the people.

c) Display NOTICES in this SECTION of the shop.

d) You need good TRAINERS to run on all TERRAINS.

e) NAMELESS SALESMEN are forever telephoning me.

f) I have a RELATION who is ORIENTAL.

g) He TRIED hard to run, but he was too TIRED.

h) She SAVES her money to buy ceramic VASES.

i) If you want to LISTEN it helps if you are SILENT.

j) The TEACHER caught the CHEATER.

k) On MONDAY we learnt about the DYNAMO.

l) Everyone AGREES that GREASE is messy.

m) Which creepy-crawly is the NICEST INSECT?

n) He saw a scary THING in the dark that NIGHT.

BRAIN WORKOUT 69
ANSWERS

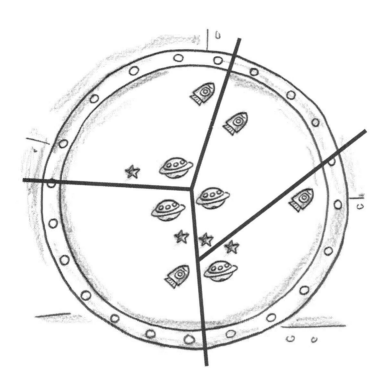

BRAIN WORKOUT 70
ANSWERS

9	8	2	1	7	3	4	6	5
7	3	6	5	4	9	2	1	8
4	7	5	2	1	8	6	3	9
5	1	8	9	6	4	3	7	2
6	9	4	3	5	2	1	8	7
3	6	1	8	2	7	9	5	4
8	2	9	7	3	6	5	4	1
2	5	3	4	8	1	7	9	6
1	4	7	6	9	5	8	2	3

BRAIN WORKOUT 71
ANSWERS

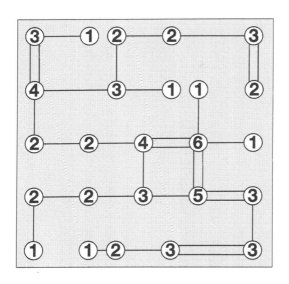

BRAIN WORKOUT 72
ANSWERS

CODE ONE

TAKE SIX STEPS EAST AND FOUR STEPS NORTH

CODE TWO

THIS IS CORRECT

CODE THREE

YOU ARE A MASTER CODE BREAKER

BRAIN WORKOUT 73
ANSWERS

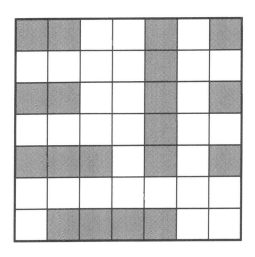

BRAIN WORKOUT 74
ANSWERS

4	1	9	7	8	3	6	5	2
2	5	3	4	1	6	7	8	9
8	6	7	9	5	2	4	1	3
3	7	4	5	9	8	2	6	1
5	9	1	6	2	4	3	7	8
6	2	8	1	3	7	5	9	4
7	8	6	2	4	9	1	3	5
1	3	2	8	6	5	9	4	7
9	4	5	3	7	1	8	2	6

BRAIN WORKOUT 75
ANSWERS

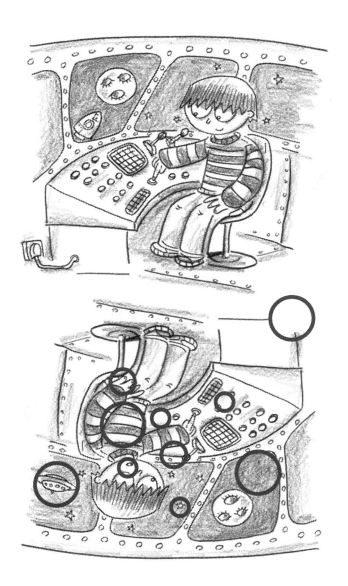

BRAIN WORKOUT 76
ANSWERS

a) 4 triangles
b) 4 quadrilaterals
c) 4 hexagons
d) 6 colours
e) 10 triangles

BRAIN WORKOUT 77
ANSWERS

Puzzle A

	6	3			
3	**1**	**2**	6		7
6	**3**	**1**	**2**	2 / 7	**2**
2	**2**	7	**1**	**2**	**4**
		8	**3**	**4**	**1**
			1	**1**	

Puzzle B

	8	2	4		
6	**1**	**2**	**3**	3	
3	**3**	3	**1**	**2**	4
6	**4**	**2**	4 / 5	**1**	**3**
	4	**1**	**3**	1	**1**
		3	**2**	**1**	

BRAIN WORKOUT 78
ANSWERS

a) Photography was introduced in the 1830s.

b) The first films with sound were released in 1926.

c) The name of the first public system for playing back films was the Kinetoscope.

d) The Lumiére brothers demonstrated the first projector system in 1895.

BRAIN WORKOUT 79
ANSWERS

Puzzle A

2	3	3	4
1	1	2	3
3	2	3	1
4	1	4	2

Puzzle B

4	3	2	1
1	1	4	2
2	4	3	4
1	4	2	2

BRAIN WORKOUT 80
ANSWERS

5	7	9	1	3	4	2	6	8
2	6	3	9	8	5	4	1	7
1	8	4	2	6	7	5	3	9
4	2	6	7	5	1	9	8	3
7	3	5	4	9	8	6	2	1
8	9	1	3	2	6	7	5	4
6	4	8	5	1	9	3	7	2
3	1	7	6	4	2	8	9	5
9	5	2	8	7	3	1	4	6

BRAIN WORKOUT 81
ANSWERS

Puzzle A

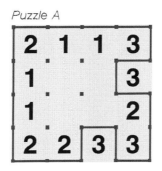

Puzzle B

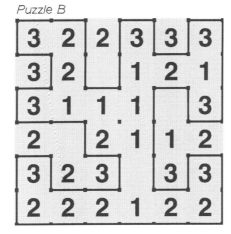

BRAIN WORKOUT 82
ANSWERS

S	S	U	B	M	I	N	O	L	U	M	U	C	C
C	U	U	L	S	S	S	U	U	O	U	O	T	R
L	S	U	T	A	R	T	S	O	B	M	I	N	T
N	U	S	M	A	S	R	M	U	S	M	U	R	T
O	T	S	O	L	R	A	I	C	L	U	O	L	S
T	A	U	T	T	T	T	R	T	C	B	A	T	M
T	R	S	A	O	C	O	S	S	M	S	T	U	T
L	T	R	T	C	O	C	M	O	M	U	M	O	S
U	S	U	L	U	M	U	C	O	R	R	I	C	L
R	O	A	I	M	T	M	C	L	C	R	R	T	U
O	T	N	L	U	B	U	L	N	M	I	I	O	M
T	L	R	U	L	M	L	I	S	L	C	O	C	T
B	A	I	L	U	T	U	A	L	C	M	C	U	U
O	S	I	S	S	I	S	U	U	L	L	C	U	U

BRAIN WORKOUT 83
ANSWERS

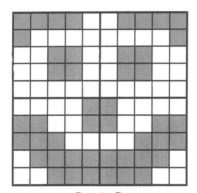

Puzzle A

Puzzle B

BRAIN WORKOUT 84
ANSWERS

CODE ONE

WELL DONE

CODE TWO

WHY DID THE COW WIN THE
NOBEL PRIZE?

CODE THREE

BECAUSE IT WAS OUTSTANDING IN
ITS FIELD!

BRAIN WORKOUT 85
ANSWERS

5	3	2	9	6	4	7	8	1
8	6	4	7	1	9	3	5	2
7	1	5	4	2	8	9	6	3
4	5	7	6	3	1	2	9	8
6	4	9	1	8	2	5	3	7
3	8	1	2	9	7	6	4	5
2	9	3	8	7	5	4	1	6
9	2	8	3	5	6	1	7	4
1	7	6	5	4	3	8	2	9

BRAIN WORKOUT 86
ANSWERS

a) 49 clocks
b) 6 clocks
c) 13 clocks
d) 29 clocks
e) 6 clocks
f) 18 different times

BRAIN WORKOUT 87
ANSWERS

a) 6 ways (1/6, 2/5, 3/4, 6/1, 5/2, 4/3)

b) The minimum total is 3
   The maximum total is 11

c) The minimum total is 7
   The maximum total is 11

d) 2, 4, 6, 8, 10

d) 3 doubles (1/1, 3/3, 5/5)

BRAIN WORKOUT 88
ANSWERS

CAT
COT
COG
DOG

HIDE
HIVE
FIVE
FINE
FIND

LOOK
COOK
COOS
COWS
SOWS
SEWS
SEES

Can you find any alternative solutions?

BRAIN WORKOUT 89
ANSWERS

BRAIN WORKOUT 90
ANSWERS

3	9	5	2	8	6	7	4	1
1	2	6	4	5	7	3	9	8
7	4	8	1	3	9	6	5	2
2	6	4	8	7	3	9	1	5
9	3	1	5	4	2	8	7	6
5	8	7	6	9	1	2	3	4
4	7	2	3	1	8	5	6	9
6	5	3	9	2	4	1	8	7
8	1	9	7	6	5	4	2	3

LOOK OUT FOR THESE TITLES!

The Kids' Book Of Sudoku
£3.99
ISBN-10: 1-905158-24-6
ISBN-13: 978-1-905158-24-9
paperback

The Kids' Book Of Kakuro
£3.99
ISBN-10: 1-905158-33-5
ISBN-13: 978-1-905158-33-1
paperback

The Kids' Book Of Hanjie
£3.99
ISBN-10: 1-905158-40-9
ISBN-13: 978-1-905158-40-8
paperback

The Kids' Book Of
Number Puzzles
£3.99
ISBN-10: 1-905158-32-7
ISBN-13: 978-1-905158-32-4
paperback

3033426R00102

Printed in Great Britain
by Amazon.co.uk, Ltd.,
Marston Gate.